THIS WE'LL DEFEND

THE WEAPONS AND EQUIPMENT OF THE
U.S. ARMY

RUSSELL PHILLIPS

SHILKA PUBLISHING
WWW.SHILKA.CO.UK

Copyright © 2013 by Russell Phillips.

All rights reserved. No part of this publication may be reproduced, distributed or transmitted in any form or by any means, including photocopying, recording, or other electronic or mechanical methods, without the prior written permission of the publisher, except in the case of brief quotations embodied in critical reviews and certain other non-commercial uses permitted by copyright law. For permission requests, write to the publisher, addressed "Attention: Permissions Coordinator," at the address below.

Shilka Publishing
Apt 2049
Chynoweth House
Trevissome Park
Truro
TR4 8UN
www.shilka.co.uk

Book Layout ©2013 BookDesignTemplates.com

Ordering Information:
Quantity sales. Special discounts are available on quantity purchases by corporations, associations, and others. For details, contact the "Special Sales Department" at the address above.

This We'll Defend/ Russell Phillips. —1st ed.
ISBN 978-0-9927648-1-4

Contents

Tracked Vehicles 1

Individual and Crew-Served Weapons 13

Helicopters 31

Surface-to-Air Missile (SAM) Systems 45

Anti-Armour Weapons 51

Indirect Fire Systems 57

Nuclear, Biological, and Chemical (NBC) Defence Equipment 77

Wheeled Vehicles 93

Digital Reinforcements: Free Ebook 113

About Russell Phillips 115

The general of the sea has need of only one science, that of navigation. The one on land has need of all, or of a talent which is the equivalent of all, that will enable him to profit by all experience, and all knowledge. A general of the sea has nothing to divine. He knows where his enemy is, he knows his strength. A general on land never knows anything with certainty, never sees his enemy well, and never knows positively where he is.

—Napoléon Bonaparte

Tracked Vehicles

> *Each war proves anew to those who may have had their doubts, the primacy of the main battle tank. Between wars, the tank is always a target for cuts. But in wartime, everyone remembers why we need it, in its most advanced, upgraded versions and in militarily significant numbers.*
>
> —IDF Brigadier General Yahuda Admon (retired)

Since their first appearance in the latter part of World War I, tanks have increasingly dominated military thinking. Armies became progressively more mechanised during World War II, with many infantry being carried in armoured carriers by the end of the war. The armoured personnel carrier (APC) evolved into the infantry fighting vehicle (IFV), which is able to support the infantry as well as simply transport them. Modern IFVs have a similar level of battlefield mobility to the tanks, allowing tanks and infantry to operate together and provide mutual support.

Abrams

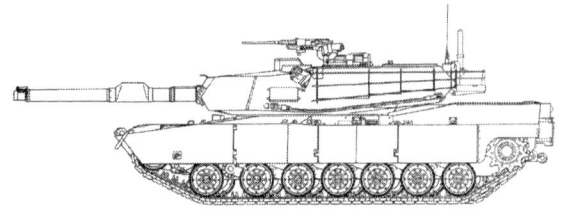

Mission

Provide heavy armour superiority on the battlefield.

Entered Army Service

1980

Description and Specifications

The Abrams tank closes with and destroys enemy forces on the integrated battlefield using mobility, fire power, and shock effect. There are three variants in service: M1A1, M1A2, and M1A2 SEP. The 120mm main gun, combined with the powerful 1,500 HP turbine engine and special armour, make the Abrams tank particularly suitable for attacking or defending against large concentrations of heavy armour forces on a highly lethal battlefield.

Features of the M1A1 modernisation program include increased armour protection; suspension improvements; and an improved nuclear, biological, and chemical (NBC) protection system that increases survivability in a contaminated environment. The M1A1D modification consists of an M1A1 with integrated computer and a far-target-designation capability. The M1A2 modernisation program includes a commander's independent thermal viewer, an improved commander's weapon station, position navigation equipment, a distributed data and power architecture, an embedded diagnostic system and improved fire-control systems.

The M1A2 System Enhancement Program (SEP) adds second-generation thermal sensors and a thermal management system. The SEP includes upgrades to processors/memory that enable the M1A2 to use the Army's common command and control software, enabling the rapid transfer of digital situational data and overlays.

M1A1

Length: 32.04 ft
Width: 12 ft
Height: 8 ft
Top Speed: 41.5 mph
Weight: 67.6 tons
Main Armament: 120mm
Crew: 4

M1A2

    Length: 32.04 ft
    Width: 12 ft
    Height: 8 ft
    Top Speed: 41.5 mph
    Weight: 68.4 tons
    Main Armament: 120mm
    Crew: 4

M1A2 SEP

    Length: 32.04 ft
    Width: 12 ft
    Height: 8 ft
    Top Speed: 42 mph
    Weight: 69.5 tons
    Main Armament: 120mm
    Crew: 4

Manufacturer

General Dynamics (Sterling Heights, MI; Warren, MI; Muskegon, MI; Scranton, PA; Lima, OH; Tallahassee, FL)

Bradley

Mission

Provides protected transport of an infantry squad on the battlefield, and supporting fire when the squad is dismounted. Also employed to suppress and defeat enemy tanks, reconnaissance vehicles, infantry fighting vehicles, armoured personnel carriers, bunkers, dismounted infantry, and attack helicopters. Performs cavalry scout and other essential missions in the 21st century (fire support and Stinger teams are carried in Bradleys). The infantry version (M2) is used most often to close with the enemy by means of fire and manoeuvre. The primary tasks performed by the cavalry version (M3) as part of a troop and/or squadron are reconnaissance, security, and flank-guard missions.

Entered Army Service

1981

Description and Specifications

The Bradley M2A3 Infantry / M3A3 Cavalry Fighting Vehicle is configured as follows:

Length: 21 ft 2 in

Width:
    11.83 ft with armour tiles
    10.75 ft without armour tiles

Height: 11.8 ft

Weight:
    50,000 lbs unloaded
    67,000 lbs combat loaded

Power Train: 600 HP Cummins VTA-903T diesel engine with GM-Allison HMPT-500-3SEC hydro-mechanical automatic transmission

Cruising Range: 250 miles

Crew:
    M2A3: 9 (3 crew; 6 dismounts)
    M3A3: 5 (3 crew; 2 dismounts)

Armament:
    25-mm M242 Bushmaster cannon
    TOW II missile system
    7.62 mm M240C machine gun

Vehicle features

Two second-generation forward looking infra-red (FLIR) sensors in the Improved Bradley Acquisition System (IBAS) and Commander's Independent Viewer (CIV) provide "Hunter-Killer target hand-off" capability with a ballistic fire-control system.

Embedded diagnostics. Integrated combat command and control (IC3) digital communications suite hosting Force XXI Battle Command Brigade-and-Below package with digital maps, messages, and friend/foe situational awareness.

Position navigation system with GPS and inertial navigation system.

Enhanced squad situational awareness with squad leader display integrated into vehicle digital images and IC3.

MANUFACTURER

United Defense, L.P. (San Jose, CA; Fayette, PA; York, PA; Arlington, VA)

Heavy Equipment Recovery Combat Utility Lift and Evacuation System (HERCULES) (M88A2)

Mission

Provide towing, winching, and hoisting to support battlefield recovery operations and evacuation of heavy tanks and other tracked combat vehicles.

Entered Army Service

1997

Description and Specifications

The M88A2 HERCULES is a full-tracked, armoured vehicle that uses the existing M88A1 chassis but significantly improves towing, winching, lifting, and braking characteristics. The HERCULES is the primary recovery support vehicle for the Abrams tank fleet, the heavy Assault Bridge, and heavy self-propelled artillery.

Length: 338 in
Height: 123 in
Width: 144 in
Weight: 70 tons
Speed:
    25 mph w/o load
    17 mph w/load
Cruising Range: 200 miles
Boom Capacity: 35 tons
Winch Capacity: 70 tons / 670 ft
Draw Bar Pull: 70 tons
Armament: One .50-calibre machine gun
Power train: 12 cylinder, 1050 HP air-cooled diesel engine with 3-speed automatic transmission
Crew: 3

MANUFACTURER

United Defense, L.P. (York, PA)

M113 Family of Vehicles

Mission

Provide a highly mobile, survivable, and reliable tracked vehicle platform that is able to keep pace with Abrams- and Bradley-equipped units and that is adaptable to a wide range of current and future battlefield tasks through the integration of specialised mission modules at minimum operational and support cost.

Entered Army Service

1960

Description and Specifications

After more than four decades, the M113 family of vehicles (FOV) is still in service in the U.S. Army (and in many foreign armies). The original M113 Armoured Personnel Carrier (APC) helped to revolutionise mobile military operations. These vehicles carried 11 soldiers plus a driver and track commander under armour protection across hostile battlefield environments. More importantly, these vehicles were air-transportable, air-droppable, and amphibious, allowing planners to incorporate APCs in a much wider range of combat situations, including many "rapid deployment" scenarios. The M113s were so successful that they were quickly identified as the foundation for a family of vehicles. Early derivatives included both command post (M577) and mortar carrier (M106) configurations.

Over the years, the M113 FOV has undergone numerous upgrades. In 1964, the M113A1 package replaced the original gasoline engine with a 212-horsepower diesel package, significantly improving survivability by eliminating the possibility of catastrophic loss from fuel tank explosions. Several new derivatives were produced, some based on the armoured M113 chassis (e.g., the M125A1 mortar carrier and M741 "Vulcan" air-defence vehicle) and some based on the unarmoured version of the chassis (e.g., the M548 cargo carrier, M667 "Lance" missile carrier, and M730 "Chaparral" missile carrier). In 1979, the A2 package of suspension and cooling enhancements was introduced.

Today's M113 fleet includes a mix of these A2 variants, together with other derivatives equipped with the most recent A3 RISE (Reliability Improvements for Selected Equipment) package. The standard RISE package includes an upgraded propulsion system (turbocharged engine and new transmission), greatly improved driver controls (new power brakes and conventional steering controls), external fuel tanks, and 200-amp alternator with four batteries. Additional A3 improvements include incorporation of spall liners and provisions for mounting external armour.

The future M113A3 fleet will include a number of vehicles that will have high-speed digital networks and data transfer systems. The M113A3 digitisation program includes applying hardware, software, and installation kits and hosting them in the M113 FOV.

CURRENT VARIANTS:

Mechanised Smoke Obscurant System
M548A1/A3 Cargo Carrier
M577A2/A3 Command Post Carrier
M901A1 Improved TOW Vehicle
M981 Fire Support Team Vehicle
M1059/A3 Smoke Generator Carrier
M1064/A3 Mortar Carrier
M1068/A3 Standard Integrated Command Post System Carrier
OPFOR Surrogate Vehicle (OSV)

MANUFACTURER

Anniston Army Depot (Anniston, AL)
United Defense, L.P. (Anniston, AL)

Individual and Crew-Served Weapons

> *Let us be clear about three facts: First, all battles and all wars are won in the end by the infantryman. Secondly, the infantryman always bears the brunt. His casualties are heavier, he suffers greater extremes of discomfort and fatigue than the other arms. Thirdly, the art of the infantryman is less stereotyped and far harder to acquire in modern war than that of any other arm.*
>
> —British Field Marshall Sir Archibald Percival Wavell

The U.S. Army's infantry use a variety of weapons, from individual weapons such as pistols and assault rifles, to crew-served weapons such as machine guns and grenade launchers. This variety of weaponry means the infantry is equipped to fight in any situation.

Bayonet

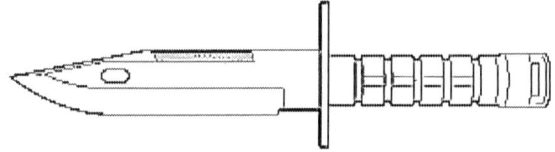

Mission

Defeat the enemy in hand-to-hand combat. Also used as a general field and utility knife.

Entered Army Service

M6: 1957
M7: 1964
M9: 1987

Description and Specifications

The M6 bayonet-knife is used as a bayonet on the M14 series rifle and as a hand weapon. The M7 bayonet-knife is used as a bayonet on the M16 series rifle, the M4 carbine and as a hand weapon. The M9 multi-purpose bayonet system is used as a bayonet on the M16 series rifle, on the M4 series carbine, as a hand weapon, as a general utility knife, as a saw and, in conjunction with its scabbard, as a wire cutter.

M6

Blade length: 6.75 in
Total length: 11.5 in

M7

Blade length: 6.5 in
Total length: 11.75 in

M9

Blade length: 7 in
Total length: 12 in

MANUFACTURER

Multiple

M4 Carbine

Photo Courtesy of PEO Soldier

Mission

Deter and, if necessary, repel adversaries by enabling individuals and small units to engage targets with accurate, lethal, direct fire.

Entered Army Service

1997

Description and Specifications

A compact version of the M16A2 rifle, with a collapsible stock, a flat-top upper receiver accessory rail and a detachable handle/rear aperture site assembly. The M4 enables a soldier operating in close quarters to engage targets at extended range with accurate, lethal fire. It achieves more than 85 percent commonality with the M16A2 rifle and replaced all .45 calibre M3 submachine guns and selected M9 pistols.

Calibre: 5.56 mm

Weight: 7.5 lbs (loaded weight with sling and one magazine)

Max. Effective Range: 600 m (area target) 500 m (point target)

MANUFACTURER

Colt Manufacturing (Hartford, CT)

M9 Pistol

Mission

Deter and, if necessary, repel adversaries by enabling individuals and small units to engage targets with accurate, lethal, direct fire.

Entered Army Service

1990

Description and Specifications

A semi-automatic, single-action/double-action pistol. The M9 is the primary side arm of the U.S. military, replacing the .45 calibre model M1911A1. The M9 has a 15-round staggered magazine with a reversible magazine release button that can be positioned for either right- or left-handed shooters.

Calibre: 9 mm
Length: 217 mm

Barrel Length: 125 mm
Weight:
    2.1 lbs (unloaded)
    2.6 lbs (fully loaded)
Range: 50 m
Manufacturer
Beretta USA

M16 Rifle

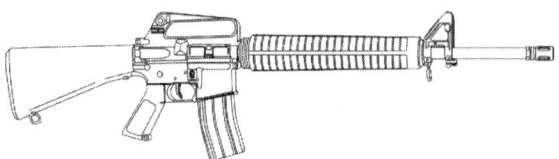

Mission

Deter and, if necessary, repel adversaries by enabling individuals and small units to engage targets with accurate, lethal, direct fire.

Entered Army Service

1964

Description and Specifications

A lightweight, air-cooled, gas-operated, magazine-fed rifle designed for either automatic or semi-automatic fire through use of a selector lever. There are four variants - the M16A1/A2/A3/A4. The M16A2 incorporates improvements in iron sight, pistol grip, stock, and overall combat effectiveness.

Accuracy is enhanced by incorporating an improved muzzle compensator, three-round burst control, and a heavier barrel; and by using the heavier NATO-standard ammunition, which is also fired by the squad automatic weapon. The M16A3 is identical to the M16A2 but has a removable carrying handle that is mounted on a Picatinny Rail (for better mounting of optics) and is without burst control. The M16A4 is identical to the M16A2 except for the removable carrying handle and Picatinny Rail.

Calibre: 5.56 mm

Weight: 8.8 lbs (including sling and one loaded magazine)

Range: 800 meters for an area target/550 meters for a point target

MANUFACTURER

Colt Manufacturing and Fabrique Nationale Manufacturing, Inc.

MK19-3 40MM Grenade Machine Gun

Mission

Deter and, if necessary, repel adversaries by enabling individuals and small units to engage targets with accurate, lethal, indirect fire.

Entered Army Service

1983

Description and Specifications

A self-powered, air-cooled, belt-fed, blowback-operated weapon designed to deliver decisive fire power against enemy personnel and lightly armoured vehicles. It replaces the M2 heavy machine guns in selected units and will be the primary suppressive weapon for combat support and combat service support units. The MK19-3 can be mounted on the HMMWV (High Mobility Multi-purpose Wheeled

Vehicle), M113 family of vehicles, five-ton trucks, and selected M88A1 recovery vehicles.

Calibre: 40 mm
Weight: 72.5 lbs
Range: 2,200 m (area target)

MANUFACTURER

General Dynamics (Saco, ME)

M203/M203A1 Grenade Launcher

Mission

Deter and, if necessary, repel adversaries by enabling individuals and small units to engage targets with accurate, lethal, grenade fire.

Entered Army Service

Early 1970s

Description and Specifications

The M203 grenade launcher is a single-shot weapon designed for use with the M16 series rifle and fires a 40mm grenade. The M203A1 grenade launcher is a single-shot weapon designed for use with the M4 series carbine and also fires a 40mm grenade. Both have a leaf sight and quadrant site. The M203 is also being used as the delivery system for a growing array of less-than-lethal munitions.

Weight:
    3 lbs (empty)
    3.6 lbs (loaded)
Overall Length: 15"
Barrel Length: 12"

Ammunition Type: CN/CS/OC tear gas rounds, smoke, non-lethal projectiles, signal, and practice rounds as well as standard 40mm rounds

Effective Range: Approximately 350 yards

MANUFACTURER

Colt Manufacturing

M240B Machine Gun

Mission

Deter and, if necessary, repel adversaries by enabling individuals and small units to engage targets with accurate, lethal, direct automatic fire.

Entered Army Service

1997

Description and Specifications

A ground-mounted, gas-operated, crew-served machine gun. This reliable 7.62mm machine gun delivers more energy to the target than the smaller calibre M249 SAW. It is issued to infantry, armour, combat engineer, Special Forces/Rangers, and selected field artillery units that require medium support fire, and has replaced the ground-mounted M60 series machine gun.

Calibre: 7.62 mm
Weight: 27.6 lbs

Max. Effective Range: 1,800 m (area target) 800 m (point target)

Rate of Fire: 200-600 rounds per minute

Manufacturer

FN Manufacturing (Columbia, SC)

M249 Squad Automatic Weapon (SAW)

Mission

Deter and, if necessary, repel adversaries by enabling individuals and small units to engage targets with accurate, lethal, direct automatic fire.

Entered Army Service

1987

Description and Specifications

A lightweight, gas-operated, one-man-portable automatic weapon capable of delivering a large volume of effective fire at ranges up to 800 meters. Two M249s are issued to each infantry squad.

Calibre: 5.56 mm
Weight: 16.5 lbs
Rate of Fire: 750 rounds per minute

Manufacturer

FN Manufacturing (Columbia, SC)

Helicopters

I wish they wouldn't land those things here while we're playing golf.

—Trapper John (M.A.S.H.)

Helicopters revolutionised warfare after World War II, as their mobility and versatility allows them to be used for a wide variety of tasks, including tank hunting, transport of troops and cargo, medical evacuation, and reconnaissance. They first saw widespread active service in Korea, and have proved their usefulness in many theatres of war since. The models currently in service with the U.S. Army are described in this section.

Apache Longbow

Mission

Conducts rear, close, and shaping missions including deep precision strike. Conducts distributed operations, precision strikes against re-locatable targets, and provides armed reconnaissance when required in day, night, obscured battlefield, and adverse weather conditions.

Entered Army Service

AH-64 (1984)
AH-64D (1998)

Description and Specifications

The AH-64 Apache is the Army's heavy division/corps attack helicopter. The AH-64D Longbow re-manufacture effort incorporates a millimetre wave fire-control radar (FCR), radar frequency interferometer (RFI), fire-and-forget radar-guided Hellfire missile and cockpit management and digitisation enhancements. The combination of the FCR, RFI, and the advanced navigation and avionics suite of the aircraft provide increased situational awareness, lethality, and survivability.

Combat Mission: 167 mph
Combat Range: 300 miles
Combat Endurance: 2.5 hours
Length: 49 ft 5 in
Mission Weight: 16,600 lbs
Armament:
    Hellfire missiles
    2.75" rockets
    30mm chain gun
Crew: 2 (pilot and co-pilot/gunner)

Manufacturer

Airframe - Boeing (Mesa, AZ)

Fire-Control Radar - Northrup Grumman (Linthicum, MD); Lockheed Martin (Owego, NY)

MTADS/PNVS - Lockheed Martin (Orlando, FL); Boeing (Mesa, AZ)

Black Hawk

Mission

Provide air assault, general support, aero-medical evacuation, command and control, and special operations support to combat and stability and support operations.

Entered Army Service

1979

Description and Specifications

The UH-60 Black Hawk is a utility tactical transport helicopter that replaces the UH-1 "Huey". The versatile Black Hawk has enhanced the overall mobility of the Army, due to dramatic improvements in troop capacity and cargo lift capability, and will serve as the Army's utility helicopter in the Objective Force. On the asymmetric battlefield, it provides the commander the agility to get to the fight quicker and to mass effects throughout the battle space across the full spectrum of conflict. An entire 11-person, fully-equipped infantry squad can be lifted in a single Black Hawk, transported faster than in predecessor systems, and in most weather conditions. The Black Hawk can reposition a 105 mm Howitzer, its crew of six, and up to 30 rounds of ammunition in a single lift. The aircraft's critical components and systems are armoured or redundant, and its airframe is designed to progressively crush on impact to protect the crew and passengers.

UH-60A

> Max. Gross Weight: 20,250 lbs
> Cruising Speed: 139 knots
> Endurance: 2.3 hours or 320 nautical miles
> External Load: 8,000 lbs
> Internal Load: 2,640 lbs (or 11 combat-equipped troops)
> Crew: 4 (2 pilots, 2 crew chiefs)
> Armament: Two 7.62mm machine guns

UH-60L

> Max. Gross Weight: 22,000 lbs, 23,500 (external cargo)
> Cruising Speed: 150 knots
> Endurance: 2.1 hours or 306 nautical miles
> External Load: 9,000 lbs
> Internal Load: 2,640 lbs (or 11 combat-equipped troops)
> Crew: 4 (2 pilots, 2 crew chiefs)
> Armament: Two 7.62mm machine guns

MANUFACTURER

United Technologies (Stratford, CT)
General Electric (Lynn, MA)

CHINOOK

MISSION

Transport ground forces, supplies, ammunition, and other battle-critical cargo in support of worldwide combat and contingency operations.

ENTERED ARMY SERVICE

1962

DESCRIPTION AND SPECIFICATIONS

The venerable twin-engine, tandem-rotor Chinook helicopter has undergone numerous upgrades since the first CH-47A model was delivered to the Army for use in Vietnam. Beginning in 1982 and ending in 1994, all CH-47A, B, and C models were upgraded to the CH-47D version, which remains the U.S. Army standard and features composite rotor blades, an improved electrical system, modularised hydraulics, triple cargo hooks, avionics, and communication improvements, and more powerful engines that can handle a 19,500 lb load – nearly twice the Chinook's original lift capacity. An upgrade program exists to re-manufacture 300 of the current fleet of 425 CH-47D's to the CH-47F standard. The MH-47E is the Special Forces variant of the Chinook and will be re-manufactured to the MH-47G.

The Chinook's cockpit accommodates two pilots and an observer. The communications suite includes jam resistant HF and UHF radio systems, and the helicopter is equipped with an Identification Friend or Foe (IFF) interrogator. Three machine guns can be mounted on the helicopter, two in the crew door on the starboard side and one window-mounted on the port side. Additionally, the helicopter is equipped with a suite of countermeasure systems, which could include one or more of the following: a missile approach warning system, jammers, radar warning system, and chaff and flare dispensers.

The Chinook has a triple hook system, which provides stability to large external loads or the capacity for multiple external loads. Large external loads such as 155mm howitzers can be transported at speeds up to 260km/h using the triple hook load configuration. Multiple external loads can be delivered to two or three separate destinations in one sortie.

The cabin provides 42 cubic meters of cargo space and 21 square meters of cargo floor area and can accommodate two HMMWVs or a HMMWV together with 105mm howitzer and gun crew. The main cabin can hold up to 33 fully-equipped troops. For medical evacuation, the cabin can accommodate 24 litters (stretchers).

Ramp operations can be carried out on water using an optional power-down ramp and water dam configuration.

The Chinook is equipped with two T55-GA-714A turbo shaft engines, which are pod-mounted on either side of the rear pylon under the rear rotor blades. The self-sealing fuel tanks are mounted in external fairings on the sides of the fuselage. The fixed tanks hold 1,030 gallons of fuel. Three additional fuel tanks can be carried in the cargo area. In-flight refuelling can extend the range of the MH-47 variant.

The CH-47F upgrade program involves the installation of a new digital cockpit and modifications to the airframe to reduce vibration. The upgraded cockpit will provide future growth potential and will include a digital data bus that permits installation of enhanced communications and navigation equipment for improved situational awareness, mission performance, and survivability. Airframe structural modifications will reduce harmful vibrations, reducing operations and support (O&S) costs and improving crew endurance. Other airframe modifications will reduce by approximately 60% the time required for aircraft tear-down and build-up after deployment on a C-5 or C-17. These modifications significantly enhance the Chinook's strategic deployment capability.

A separate but complementary effort involves the installation of more powerful and reliable T55-GA-714A engines that improve fuel efficiency and enhance lift performance by approximately 3,900 lbs (enabling it to carry the M198 155mm towed howitzer). Installation of an improved crash-worthy extended range fuel system (ERFS II) will enable Chinook self-deployment and extend the operational radius of all other missions. A program is also under way to reduce O&S costs through the joint development with the United Kingdom of a low-maintenance rotor hub.

    Max. Gross Weight: 50,000 lbs
    Empty Weight: 23,401 lbs
    Max. Speed: 170 knots
    Normal Cruise Speed: 130 knots
    Rate of Climb: 1,522 ft/min
    Rotor System: three manual-folding blades per hub (two hubs); 225 revolutions per minute; 60-ft rotor span
    Troop Capacity: 36 (33 troops plus 3 crew members)
    Litter Capacity: 24
    Sling-load Capacity:
        26,000 lb centre hook
        17,000 lb forward/aft hook
        25,000 lb tandem
    Minimum Crew: 3 (pilot, co-pilot, and flight engineer)

Manufacturer

    Aircraft - Boeing (Philadelphia, PA)
    Cockpit Upgrade - Rockwell Collins (Cedar Rapids, IA)
    Engine Upgrade - Honeywell (Phoenix, AZ)
    ERFS II - Robertson Aviation (Tempe, AZ)

Kiowa Warrior

Mission

Conduct armed reconnaissance, security, target acquisition and designation, command and control, light attack, and defensive air combat missions in support of combat and contingency operations. Replaces AH-1 Cobra attack helicopters (those that function as scouts in air cavalry troops and light attack companies) and OH-58A and C Kiowas in air cavalry troops.

Entered Army Service

1991

Description and Specifications

A single engine, four-bladed helicopter with advanced visionics, navigation, communication, and weapons and cockpit integration systems. The mast-mounted sight (MMS) houses a thermal imaging system, low-light television, laser range finder/designator, and an optical boresight system. These systems enable the Kiowa Warrior to operate by day and night and allow target acquisition and engagement at stand-off ranges and in adverse weather conditions. The Kiowa Warrior's highly accurate navigation system provides precise target location that can be sent digitally to other aircraft or artillery via its advanced digital communications system. Battlefield imagery can be transmitted to provide near-real-time situational awareness to command and control elements. The Laser Designator can provide autonomous designation for the Laser Hellfire or remote designation for other laser-guided precision weapons.

The Kiowa Warrior is equipped with two universal quick-change weapons pylons. Each pylon can be armed with two Hellfire missiles, seven Hydra 70 rockets, two air-to-air Stinger missiles, or one .50 calibre fixed forward machine gun. The armament systems combine to provide anti-armour, anti-personnel, and anti-aircraft capabilities at stand-off ranges.

The Kiowa Warrior is rapidly deployable by air and can be fully operational within minutes of arrival. Two Kiowa aircraft can be transported in a C-130 aircraft. For air transportation the vertical tail fin pivots, the main rotor blades and the horizontal stabiliser are folded, and the mast mounted sight, IFF antenna, and lower wire cutter are removed. The landing gear can kneel to decrease the height.

Crew: 2
Max. Gross Weight: 5,500 lbs (armed)
Empty Weight: 3,289 lbs
Height: 12 ft, 10.6 in
Width: 6 ft, 5.4 in

Length: 33 ft, 4 in
Rotor Diameter: 35 ft
Max. Cruise Speed: 128 mph
Range: 299 miles (sea level, no weapons, 10% reserve)
Ceiling: 19,000 ft
Armament:
    Air-to-air Stinger (ATAS) (2-round launcher)
    .50 calibre machine gun (500 rounds)
    Hydra 70 (2.75 in) rockets (7-shot pod)
    Hellfire missiles (2-round launcher)

MANUFACTURER

Rolls Royce/Allison Engines (Indianapolis, IN)
Honeywell (Albuquerque, NM)
Bell Helicopter, Textron (Fort Worth, TX)
Boeing (Anaheim, CA)
Simula (Tempe, AZ)
Edwards (Bristol, TN)

Surface-to-Air Missile (SAM) Systems

> *The mission of air defense artillery is to protect the force and selected geopolitical assets from aerial attack, missile attack, and surveillance.*
>
> —U.S. Army Field Manual FM 44-44: Avenger Platoon, Section, and Squad Operations

The U.S. Army is fully aware of how useful helicopters and fixed-wing aircraft can be in support of ground troops. The Avenger and Patriot surface-to-air missile systems are employed to prevent an enemy from making good use of such support.

Avenger

Mission

Provide mobile, short-range air defence protection against cruise missiles, unmanned aerial vehicles, low-flying fixed-wing aircraft, and helicopters to divisions, armoured cavalry regiments, separate brigades, and corps/theatre air defence brigades.

Entered Army Service

1989

Description and Specifications

The system consists of a gyro-stabilised air defence turret mounted on a modified heavy HMMWV. The turret has two Stinger missile launcher pods, each capable of firing up to four fire-and-forget infra-red/ultraviolet guided missiles in rapid succession. Avenger can be linked to the Forward Area Air Defence Command, Control,

Communications and Intelligence (FAAD C3I) system, which permits external radar tracks and messages to be passed to the fire unit to alert and cue the gunner. Using the newly developed Slew-to-Cue subsystem, the commander or gunner can select a FAAD C3I reported target for engagement from a display, then, by a single push-button, initiate an automatic slew in azimuth.

Weapons: Eight ready-to-fire Stinger missiles, One .50-calibre machine gun

Sensors: Forward Looking Infra-red (FLIR) sensor/laser range finder/optical sight

Length: 16 ft 3 in

Weight: 8,600 lbs

Crew: 2

Manufacturer

Boeing (Huntsville, AL)
AM General (South Bend, IN)

Patriot

Mission

Provide defence of critical assets and manoeuvre forces belonging to the corps and to echelons above corps against aircraft, cruise missiles, and tactical ballistic missiles.

Entered Army Service

1985

Description and Specifications

The combat element of the PATRIOT (Phased Array Tracking Intercept of Target) missile system is the fire unit, which consists of a phased array radar set, and engagement control station, an electric power plant, an antenna mast group, a communications relay group, and up to eight launching stations.

The radar set provides all tactical functions of airspace surveillance, target detection, identification, classification and tracking, and missile guidance and engagement support. The engagement control station provides the human interface for command and control of operations. Each launching station contains four ready-to-fire PAC-2, guidance enhanced missiles (GEM, GEM+) sealed in canisters that function as both shipping containers and launch tubes.

The Patriot Advanced Capability-3 (PAC-3) upgrade program incorporates significant upgrades to the radar set and engagement control station, and adds the new PAC-3 missile, which utilises hit-to-kill technology for greater lethality against tactical ballistic missiles armed with weapons of mass destruction. Additionally, up to 16 PAC-3 missiles can be loaded per launcher, increasing fire power and missile defence capabilities.

Manufacturer

Raytheon (Bedford, MA)
Lockheed Martin (Grand Prairie, TX)

Anti-Armour Weapons

> *If the target is identified as enemy, he [the gunner] places the cross-hairs on the center mass of the exposed portion of the target, presses the trigger, and smoothly tracks the target until missile impact.*
>
> —U.S. Army Field Manual FM 23-34: TOW Weapon Systems

Modern armies are reliant on a variety of armoured vehicles, from tanks to armoured personnel carriers and infantry fighting vehicles. The U.S. Army introduced the Rocket Launcher, M1 (more commonly known as the "Bazooka") shoulder-fired anti-tank weapon during World War II. Since then, the concept has been improved, and the modern U.S. infantryman now has access to anti-tank missiles with advanced guidance systems.

Javelin

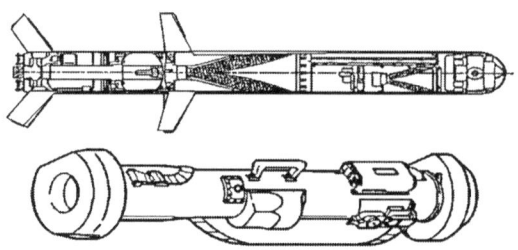

Mission

Provide a man-portable, highly lethal medium anti-tank weapon system to the infantry, scouts, and combat engineers.

Entered Army Service

1996

Description and Specifications

Javelin is the first "fire-and-forget" shoulder-fired anti-tank missile now fielded to the U.S. Army and U.S. Marine Corps, replacing Dragon. Javelin's top-attack flight mode, superior self-guiding tracking system and advanced warhead design allows it to defeat all known tanks out to ranges of 2500m.

Javelin's two major components are a reusable command launch unit (CLU) and a missile sealed in a disposable launch tube assembly. The CLU's integrated day/night sight provides target engagement capability in adverse weather and countermeasure environments. The CLU also may be used by itself for battlefield surveillance and reconnaissance. Javelin is fielded with no specific test measurement or diagnostic equipment - allowing forces to deploy rapidly and unencumbered.

Javelin's fire-and-forget guidance mode enables gunners to fire and then immediately take cover, greatly increasing survivability. Special features include a selectable top-attack or direct-fire mode (for targets under cover or for use in urban terrain against bunkers and buildings), target lock-on before launch, and a very limited back-blast that enables gunners to safely fire from enclosures and covered fighting positions.

Javelin can also be installed on tracked, wheeled, or amphibious vehicles.

Weight (missile and CLU): 49.5 lbs

Length Overall: 3 ft 6 in

Range: In excess of 2500m

Crew: 2

Manufacturer

A joint venture between Raytheon (Tucson, AZ) and Lockheed Martin (Orlando, FL)

TOW

MISSION

Defeat armoured vehicles and urban enclosed threats at extended ranges in all expected battlefield conditions.

ENTERED ARMY SERVICE

1970

DESCRIPTION AND SPECIFICATIONS

The TOW (Tube-launched, Optically-tracked, Wire command-link guided) Missile System consists of a tripod, traversing unit, missile guidance set, launch tube, optical sight, battery assembly, and any of five missile variations. The TOW missile system also includes a thermal sight that provides a capability for operations at night, in reduced visibility, and in a countermeasure environment. TOW missiles are all-up rounds encased in a disposable container.

The TOW system is mounted on various platforms including the Bradley Fighting Vehicle, the improved TOW vehicle and the HMMWV. In addition, it can be operated in a dismounted ground mode. The TOW is guided to its target merely by the gunner keeping the cross-hairs on the target. Corrective information is sent to the missile by two thin wires that deploy in flight.

Since initial fielding, five variations of the missile and two variations of the TOW subsystem have been fielded. In FY92 the direct-attack TOW 2A missile was replaced as the standard production missile by the top-attack TOW 2B missile—both are in use.

Missile Weight: TOW 2A: 47.1 lbs; TOW 2B: 49.8lbs

Missile Length: 46.1 in

Min. Range: TOW 2A: 65 m; TOW 2B: 200 m

Max. Range: 3,750 m

Launcher Weight with TOW 2 Mods: 204.6 lb

Crew: 2

MANUFACTURER

Hughes (missiles)
Hughs and Kollsman (night sights)
Electro Design Mfg. (launchers)

Indirect Fire Systems

God fights on the side with the best artillery

—Napoléon Bonaparte

Artillery has been a feature of the battlefield ever since gunpowder was invented. In the days of Napoléon, the artillery would deploy alongside the infantry and cavalry. Nowadays, however, the artillery can be deployed far to the rear, with forward observers on the front line to direct the artillery's fire via radio link.

MLRS

Mission

Provide counter fire and suppression of enemy air defences, light materiel, and personnel targets at ranges from 15 to 300+ kilometres.

Entered Army Service

1983

Description and Specifications

The MLRS (Multiple Launch Rocket System) is a high-mobility automatic system based on an M270 weapons platform. The MLRS is capable of supporting and delivering all free-flight basic and extended-range (ER-MLRS) rockets and the Army Tactical Missile System (ATACMS) Block I missiles.

The MLRS launcher unit comprises an M270 launcher loaded with 12 rockets, packaged in two six-rocket pods. The launcher, which is mounted on a stretched Bradley chassis, is a highly automated self-loading and self-aiming system. It contains a fire-control computer that integrates the vehicle and rocket-launching operations. Without leaving the cab, the crew of three (driver, gunner, and section chief) can fire up to twelve MLRS rockets in less than 60 seconds.

Length: 22.4 ft
Width: 9.8 ft
Height: 8.5 ft
Weight: 54,500 lbs
Range: 300 miles
Speed: 40 mph
Crew: 3

MANUFACTURER

Lockheed Martin (Dallas, TX)

Towed Howitzer (105 mm) M102

Mission

Provide destructive, suppressive, and protective indirect and direct artillery fire in support of combined arms operations.

Entered Army Service

1964

Description and Specifications

The M102 105mm towed howitzer is a lightweight towed weapon that provides direct support fires to light, airborne, and air assault forces. It can be towed by a 2-ton truck or HMMWV, dropped by parachute or transported with its basic load of ammunition by UH60 or larger helicopter and C130 aircraft. It is nearly three-quarters of a ton lighter than the World War II-era M101A1 105mm towed howitzer that it replaced. When emplaced, the howitzer's high volume of fire compensates in large measure for the lower explosive weight of the projectile compared to the 155mm howitzers. It has a very low silhouette when firing and a roller tyre attached to the trail assembly of the M102 permits the weapon to be rotated 360 degrees around a firing platform, which provides the pivot for the weapon. The weapon can be elevated from -5 degrees to a maximum of 75 degrees. The M102 has been replaced in the active Army by the M119A1 105mm towed howitzer. The M102 is still found in several U.S. Army National Guard units and the U.S. Air Force uses the same cannon and recoil system in the AC130 gunship.

Length: 17.1 ft

Width: 6.4 ft

Height: 5.2 ft

Weight: 3,004 lbs

Crew: 8

Range: 11,500 m standard; 15,100 m rocket-assisted

Max. Rate of Fire: 10 rounds per minute for first 3 minutes

Sustained Rate of Fire: 3 rounds per minute

Ammunition: The M102 fires all standard NATO 105mm ammunition, but not the newer extended range ammunition

MANUFACTURER

Rock Island Arsenal

Towed Howitzer (105mm) M119A1/A2

Mission

Provide destructive, suppressive, and protective indirect and direct artillery fire in support of combined arms operations.

Entered Army Service

1989

Description and Specifications

The M119A1/A2 105mm towed howitzer is a lightweight towed weapon that provides direct support fires to light, airborne, and air assault forces. The prime mover for the M119 is the HMMWV. However, it can be dropped by parachute or airlifted with its basic load of ammunition by UH60 and CH47 helicopters or C130 aircraft. The M119A1 and the product-improved M119A2 provide significantly greater range and lethality than the M101A1 and M102 howitzers.

Based on the L118 British Light Gun, the M119 systems in U.S. units have a digital fire-control system. The Light Artillery System Improvement Program (LASIP) Block I improvements, initiated in 1998, provided a new low-temperature recuperator, which increased low-temperature capability (from -25 F to -50 F), increased brake diameter from 11" to 12", improved interchangeability of spare/repair parts, simplified tail light assembly, improved trail access cover, reduced maintenance on the elevating clutch, increased trail life, and added brackets to incorporate a chronograph and battery computer system. Block I improved howitzers were re-designated as the M119A1.

Additional LASIP improvements in Block II included a redesigned elevation gearbox, removal of radioactive tritium from the fire-control system, installation of a new buffer with improved seals and no compensating tubes, simplified oil filling and monitoring hardware, addition of a roll bar to reduce damage during air drop, and an improved rammer/extractor tool. Howitzers with Block II applied are designated as M119A2.

Length: 20.75 ft
Width: 5.83 ft
Height: 7.25 ft
Weight: 4,270 lbs
Crew: 7
Range: 14,000 m standard; 19,500 m rocket-assisted
Max. Rate of Fire: 6 rounds per minute for first 2 minutes

Sustained Rate of Fire: 3 rounds per minute

Ammunition: The M119A1/A2 fires all standard NATO 105mm artillery ammunition, including the M1 High Explosive, M314 Illuminating, M60/M60A2 White Phosphorous (smoke). In addition, it fires the M913 and M760 extended range ammunition.

Manufacturer

Joint U.S./RO Partnerships (Rock Island Arsenal, Watervliet Arsenal, Seller Instruments, and Royal Ordnance, U.K.)

Towed Howitzer (155mm) M198

Mission

Provide destructive, suppressive, and protective indirect and direct artillery fire in support of combined arms operations.

Entered Army Service

1978

Description and Specifications

The M198 155mm towed howitzer is a medium artillery system that provides direct support fires on an interim basis to the Stryker Brigade Combat Teams and direct general support fires to light and special purpose forces (Airborne and Air Assault). As the successor to the older M114A1 155mm towed system fielded in World War II, the M198 provides significant improvements in lethality, range, reliability, availability, emplacement, and movement. Normally towed by a five-ton truck, the M198 system can also be dropped by parachute or transported by a CH47 Chinook helicopter or C130 aircraft.

The carriage of the M198 has a retractable suspension system and a top carriage which can be rotated 180 degrees to decrease overall length for shipment or storage. The fire-control equipment may be used by one or two crewmen for direct or indirect fire. The gunner on the left side controls left and right (traversing) settings and the assistant gunner on the right side controls up and down (elevation) settings.

Length: 40.7 feet (in tow); 36.2 feet (firing)

Width: 9.2 feet (in tow)

Height: 9.5 feet (in tow)

Weight: 16,000 lbs

Crew: 10

Range: 22,400 m standard; 30,000 m rocket-assisted

Max. Rate of Fire: 4 rounds per minute for first 2 minutes

Sustained Rate of Fire: 2 rounds per minute

Ammunition: The M198 can fire all current 155mm NATO-standard ammunition, including high explosive (HE), smoke (HC, WP), dual-purpose improved conventional munitions (DPICM), family of scatterable mines (FASCAM), cannon-launched guided projectiles (Copperhead), and illumination. The HE round weighs 95 pounds.

MANUFACTURER

Rock Island Arsenal

M120/M121 Mortar

Mission

Provide heavy weapon, high-angle organic indirect fire support to the manoeuvre unit commander.

Entered Army Service

1990

Description and Specifications

A conventional smoothbore, muzzle-loaded mortar system that provides increased range, lethality, and safety compared to the World War II-vintage 4.2-inch (107mm) heavy mortar system it replaced in mechanised infantry, motorised, armoured, and cavalry units. It is employed in towed (M120) and carrier-mounted (M121) versions and in the Stryker Brigade Combat Team mortar carrier. It fires a family of enhanced, U.S.-produced ammunition. The M120 towed system consists of the M298 Cannon (tube), M190 Bipod, M9 Baseplate, and the M67 Sight Unit. The M121 tracked carrier version consists of the M298 Cannon, M191 Bipod, M9 Baseplate, and the Carrier Adaption Kit. With the use of an auxiliary M9 Baseplate and extension feet for the M191 Bipod, the M121 can be dismounted from the vehicle and emplaced for ground-mounted operation.

Calibre: 120mm

Cannon Length: 69 in (1.75 m)

Maximum Range: 7,240 m

Minimum Range: 200 m

Weight: 319 lbs

Rate of Fire: 16 rounds per minute for the first minute; 4 rounds per minute sustained

Ammunition: High-explosive, smoke, illumination (visible light and infra-red), full-range practice

Crew: 4 (M121 carrier-mounted on the M1064); 5 (M120 towed)

MANUFACTURER

Multiple

M224 Mortar

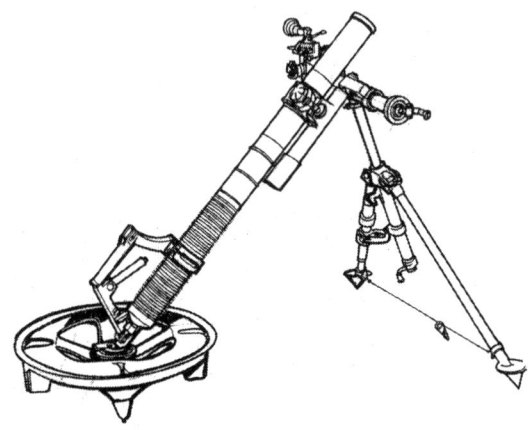

Mission

Provide long-range indirect fire support to airborne, air assault, light infantry, mountain, and special operations forces.

Entered Army Service

1978

Description and Specifications

The M224 is a high-angle weapon used for close-in support of ground troops. The M224 system consists of the M25 Cannon (tube), M170 Bipod, M7 Baseplate for conventional mode firing or M8 Baseplate for hand-held mode firing, and the M64A1 Sight Unit. This smooth bore system can be gravity-fired or fired by using a manual spring-loaded firing system.

Calibre: 60mm

Cannon Length: 40 in (1.02 m)

Max. Range: 3,490 m (conventional); 1,340 m (hand held)

Min. Range: 70 m (conventional); 75 m (hand held)

Weight: 48 lbs (conventional); 18 lbs (hand held)

Rate of Fire: (dependent on ammunition round fired) Max.: 18-30 per minute for 1 to 4 minutes; Sustained: 8 to 20 per minute

Ammunition: High-explosive / multi-option fuse, high-explosive point detonating fuse, white phosphorous/smoke, and illumination

Crew: 3

Manufacturer

Multiple

M252 Mortar

Photograph by Lance Corporal Dan Hosack

Mission

Provide long-range indirect fire support to light infantry, air assault, and airborne units across the entire battalion front with sufficient range to engage targets out to the limit of the battalion zone of influence.

Entered Army Service

1987

Description and Specifications

The M252 81mm mortar is a crew-served, medium weight mortar which is highly accurate and provides for a greater range and lethality than the previous 81mm mortar. The M252 system consists of the M253 Cannon (tube), M177 Mortar Mount, M3A1 Baseplate, and M64A1 Sight Unit.

Calibre: 81mm

Cannon Length: 50 in (1.27 m)
Max. Range: 5,935 m
Min. Range: 83 m
Weight: 91 lbs
Rate of Fire: (dependent on ammunition round fired) Max.: 25-30 per minute for 2 minutes; Sustained: 8 to 16 per minute
Ammunition: A variety of NATO-standard ammunition, including high-explosive, red phosphorous/smoke, and illumination
Crew: 3

MANUFACTURER

Multiple

Paladin

Mission

Provide the primary artillery support for armoured and mechanised infantry divisions.

Entered Army Service

1963 (M109)

Description and Specifications

The M109A6 (Paladin) howitzer is the most technologically advanced self-propelled cannon system in The U.S. Army. The "A6" designation identifies several changes to the standard model that provide improvements to weapon survivability, responsiveness, reliability, availability, maintainability, armament, and terminal effects.

The fire-control system is fully automated, providing accurate position location, azimuth reference and on-board ballistic solutions of fire missions. The howitzer has a servo-driven, computer-controlled gun drive with manual backup. Paladin uses state-of-the-art components to achieve dramatic improvements in the following:

Survivability: "Shoot and scoot" tactics; improved ballistic and nuclear, biological, and chemical protection.

Responsive fires: Capable of firing within 45 seconds from complete stop with on-board communications, remote travel lock and automated cannon slew capability.

Accurate fires: On-board POSNAV and technical fire control.

Extended range: 30 km with HE rocket-assisted projectile (RAP) and M203 propellant.

Increased reliability: Improved engine, track, and diagnostics.

Upgrades include: Global positioning system aided self-location, M93 Muzzle Velocity System, and commercial off-the-shelf based computer processor.

Max. Unassisted Range: 22,000 m

Max. Rocket-Assisted Range: 30,000 m

Min. Range: 4,000 m

Max. Rate of Fire: 4 rounds/minute for three minutes

Max. Rate of Fire: 1 round/minute (dependent on thermal warning devices)

Weight (empty): 56,400 lbs

Weight (combat loaded): Approximately 63,615 lbs

Crew: 4 (crew of accompanying M992 FAASV: 5)

MANUFACTURER

United Defence, L.P. (York, PA)
TRW (Carson City, CA)

Nuclear, Biological, and Chemical (NBC) Defence Equipment

> *When you see something that is technically sweet, you go ahead and do it and argue about what to do about it only after you've had your technical success. That is the way it was with the atomic bomb.*
>
> —J. Robert Oppenheimer, testifying in his defence during his 1954 security hearings

Since World War I, the U.S. Army has not had to fight on a battlefield contaminated with nuclear, chemical or biological agents, but it trains and equips its soldiers to be prepared for such a possibility.

Field Protective Mask, M40/M42-Series

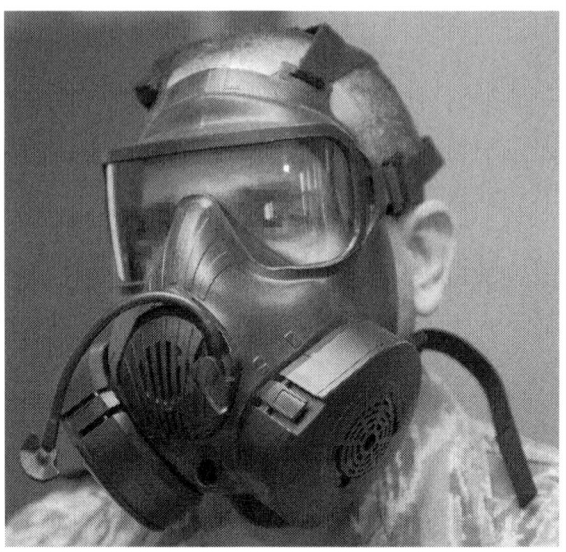

Mission

Provide respiratory, eye, and face protection against chemical and biological agents, radioactive fallout particles, and battlefield contaminants.

Entered Army Service

1992

Description and Specifications

The M40-series protective masks replace the M17-series protective mask as the standard Army field mask, providing improved comfort, fit, and protection. The mask consists of a silicone rubber face piece with an in-turned peripheral face seal, binocular rigid eye lens system and elastic head harness. Other features include front and side voicemitters, allowing better communication particularly when operating FM communications equipment, drink tube for a drinking capability while being worn, clear and tinted inserts, and a filter canister with NATO standard threads. Because of these features, the mask can be worn continuously for 8 to 12 hours.

The face-mounted canister (gas and aerosol filter) can be worn on either the left or the right cheek, and will withstand a maximum of 15 nerve, choking, and blister agent attacks. It will also withstand a maximum of two blood agent attacks. Biological agents do not degrade the filter.

The M40A1 is the mask issued to dismounted soldiers. It is available in small, medium, and large sizes.

The M42A2 Combat Vehicle Crewman Mask has the same components as the M40A1 with an additional built-in microphone for wire communication. The filter canister is attached to the end of the hose with an adaptor for the CPFU connection.

The M45 Protective Mask, issued to Blackhawk crew members, provides protection without the aid of forced ventilation air. It is compatible with aircraft sighting systems and night vision devices. It has close fitting eyepieces, a voicemitter, drink tube, and a low-profile filter canister.

The M48 and M49 masks, issued to Apache aviators, are an upgrade of the M43 Type I mask. Their improved blower is chest-mounted, lighter, less bulky, and battery powered.

Several mask improvements have been introduced over the years through Pre-Planned Product Improvement (P3I) Programs, which resulted in the M40A1 and M40A2 configurations. The improvements include a quick-doff hood, second skin, canister interoperability (M42A1 only), and voice amplification (M7), new nose cup, two new carriers, and improved vision correction. An additional product improvement was adopted in late 1994, which upgraded the M42 to the M42A2 configuration. This change provides a detachable microphone that improves reliability, simplifies production, and permits field replacements.

MANUFACTURER

ILC Dover (Frederica, Delaware)

Nuclear, Biological, and Chemical Reconnaissance System M93/M93A1

Mission

Detect, identify, and mark areas of nuclear and chemical contamination; sample soil, water, and vegetation for nuclear, biological, and chemical (NBC) contamination; and report accurate information to supported commanders in real time.

Entered Army Service

1998

Description and Specifications

A fully integrated NBC reconnaissance system with a dedicated system of NBC detection, warning, and sampling equipment integrated into a six-wheeled, all-wheel-drive armoured vehicle. This system is also referred to as the "Fox NBC Reconnaissance System".

Originally developed by the Germans for use by their military, the U.S. requirement for the Fox system was generated in the late 1980s in response to a perceived need to quickly field a chemical reconnaissance vehicle to U.S. forces in Europe. The NBCRS Non-Developmental Item Program consists of three acquisition phases. The Interim System Production phase provided 48 urgently needed German-produced vehicles (designated the XM93) that met many of the U.S. requirements. As part of this phase, the German government donated an additional 60 "Americanised" XM93 vehicles to the U.S. in support of Operation Desert Storm. The Block 1 modification phase upgraded all XM93 vehicles to the M93A1 configuration. The first U.S. unit was equipped with the NBCRS-Fox Block 1 system (M93A1) in October 1998.

The M93A1 contains an enhanced NBC sensor suite consisting of the M21 Remote Sensing Chemical Agent Alarm (RSCAAL), MM1 Mobile Mass Spectrometer, Chemical Agent Monitor/Improved Chemical Agent Monitor (CAM/ICAM), AN/VDR-2 Beta Radiac, and M22 Automatic Chemical Agent Detector/Alarm (ACADA). The NBC sensor suite has been digitally linked with the communications and navigation subsystems by a dual-purpose central processor system known as the Multi-purpose Integrated Chemical Agent Detector (MICAD). The MICAD processor fully automates NBC warning and reporting functions and provides the crew commander with full situational awareness of the Fox's NBC sensors, navigation, and communications systems. The M93A1 Fox is also equipped with an advanced position navigation system (Global Positioning System [GPS] and the Autonomous Navigation System [ANAV]) which enables the system to accurately locate and report agent contamination. It has an over-pressure filtration system that permits the crew to operate in a shirt-sleeve environment that is fully protected from the effects of NBC agents and contamination outside the vehicle. The automated features of the M93A1 reduce the crew requirements to three soldiers from the four soldiers required to operate the M93 Fox.

The M93A1 is capable of detecting chemical contamination in its immediate environment through point detection and at a distance through the use of the M21 RSCAAL. The Fox system automatically integrates contamination information from sensors with input from on-board navigation and meteorological systems and rapidly transmits via SINCGARS radios its digital NBC warning messages to warn follow-on forces. Two Reconnaissance systems, working as a team, will normally precede the movement of troops and materiel to locate and mark contaminated areas.

The Fox system is fully amphibious, with swimming speeds up to six miles per hour.

Weight: 17 tons
Length: 22.25 ft
Height: 8.1 ft
Max. Speed: 65 mph on-road
Power plant: Mercedes-Benz OM 402A V-8 diesel
Horsepower: 320 HP
Crew: 3
Basis of Issue: 6 per recon platoon (1 platoon per heavy division); 6 per ACR; 1 per separate brigade; additional assets at Corps level

Manufacturer

General Dynamics Land Systems (Detroit, MI; Anniston, AL)

Henschel Wehrtechnik (Kassel, Germany)

Chemical Agent Detector Kit, M256A1

Mission

Detect and identify blood, blister, and nerve agents present either as liquid or as vapour. May be used to determine when it is safe to unmask, to locate and identify chemical hazards (reconnaissance), and to monitor decontamination effectiveness. The M256 is not an alarm; it is a tool used after soldiers have received other warnings about the possible presence of chemical warfare agents, and have responded by putting on their chemical protective clothing.

Entered Army Service

1978

Description and Specifications

The M256 consists of a carrying case, a booklet of M8 paper, 12 disposable sampler-detectors individually sealed in a plastic laminated foil envelope, and a set of instruction cards attached by a lanyard to the plastic carrying case. The case is made from moulded, high-impact plastic and has a nylon carrying strap and a nylon belt attachment. The case measures seven inches high, five inches wide, and three inches in depth. The entire kit weighs 1.2 pounds. The kit can operate in temperatures ranging from minus 25 degrees Fahrenheit (-32 degrees Celsius) to 120 degrees Fahrenheit (49 degrees Celsius).

The M8 paper is used to test liquid substances for the presence of nerve agents and blister agents. It is similar to the litmus (pH) paper that is found in almost any laboratory in that a test result is indicated in both types of paper by a change in colour. The difference is that M8 paper is specifically designed (dye-impregnated) to react to nerve agents and blister agents in liquid form (M8 paper is also issued to soldiers as a separate piece of chemical detection equipment). The soldier blots the M8 paper on a suspected liquid agent and observes for colour change. There is a colour chart inside the front cover of the booklet for comparison. The M8 paper comes in 4" x 2.5" booklets, each containing 25 sheets of detector paper.

Each sampler-detector contains a square impregnated spot for blister agents, a circular test spot for blood agents, a star test spot for nerve agents, and a lewisite detecting tablet and rubbing tab. The test spots are made of standard laboratory filter paper. There are eight glass ampoules, six containing reagents for testing and two in an attached chemical heater. When the ampoules are crushed between the fingers, formed channels in the plastic sheets direct the flow of liquid reagent to wet the test spots. Each test spot or detecting tablet develops a distinctive colour which indicates whether a chemical agent is or is not present in the air. The use of eel enzyme for the nerve test in place of horse enzyme provides for an improvement to the M256A1 kit by detecting lower levels of nerve agent. Any type of mustard is also detectable as long as vapour is present.

By following the directions on the foil packets or in the instruction booklet, a soldier can conduct a complete test with the liquid-sensitive M8 paper and the vapour-sensitive sampler-detector in approximately 20 minutes.

A M256A1 trainer simulator was developed to provide realistic training while avoiding unnecessary exposure to potentially carcinogenic reagents in the M256A1 detector kit. The M256A1 trainer contains 36 pre-engineered detector tickets and an instruction booklet. The pre-engineered detector tickets show colour changes comparable to those seen when the M256A1 detector kit is used in clean or contaminated environments.

MANUFACTURER

Multiple

Joint Service Lightweight Integrated Suit Technology (JSLIST)

Mission

When combined with the Chemical Protective Mask, the JSLIST provides protection against chemical and biological agents, radioactive fallout particles, and battlefield contaminants.

Entered Army Service

1997

Description and Specifications

The JSLIST is the product of a four-service effort to field a common chemical protective clothing ensemble including a lightweight protective garment, multi-purpose overboots, and gloves. Each component is based on state-of-the-art materiel technologies that have undergone extensive user evaluation and field and laboratory testing. JSLIST Program objectives included reduced heat stress, compatibility with all interfacing equipment, longer wear, and washability. The JSLIST replaces the Battle Dress Overgarment (BDO).

The JSLIST overgarment is a universal, lightweight, two-piece, front-opening suit that can be worn as an overgarment or as a primary uniform over underwear. It has an integral hood, bellows-type sockets, high-waist trousers, adjustable suspenders, adjustable waistband, and a waist-length jacket that enhances system comfort, improves system acceptance and maximises compatibility with the individual user equipment.

Apart from the integral hood, on the waist-long coat, a flap fastened with Velcro covers the zip. The sleeves also have Velcro wrist-closure adjustment tabs, and the left sleeve has an outside expandable pocket with flap.

The JSLIST liner consists of a non-woven front, laminated to activate carbon spheres and bonded to a knitted back that absorbs chemical agents. Previously, the BDO liner consisted of charcoal-impregnated polyurethane foam and nylon tricot laminate. The BDO foam deteriorated as the soldiers rubbed against it, which could become messy.

The bulky charcoal layer found in the older BDOs is replaced by air-permeable fabric made with highly specialised activated carbon spherical absorbers, which is lighter, cooler, and provides a higher level of protection without blocking the movement of air and perspiration through the suit. More perspiration will also be able to escape. Weighing just under six pounds, the new suit is about half the weight of the BDO. It is available in four-colour Woodland or a three-colour Desert Camouflage pattern. It can be worn in an uncontaminated environment for 45 days with up to six launderings or for over 120 days with no launderings. The JSLIST can be worn in a contaminated environment for 24 hours. Each soldier is issued two JSLIST.

The Multi-purpose Rain/Snow/CB Overboot (MULO) replaces the older black vinyl overboot/green vinyl overboot (BVO/GVO). The MULO is made by injection moulding an elastomer blend, compounded to provide the characteristic chemical and environmental protection required. It incorporates two quick-release side buckles and is designed to be worn over the standard issue combat boot, jungle boot, and intermediate cold/wet boot. The MULO provides 60 days of durability and 24 hours of protection against liquid chemical agents. The MULO is capable of being decontaminated to an operationally safe level using standard field decontaminates. Environmental protection is provided against water, snow, and mud, in addition to petroleum, oil, and lubricant (POL) and flame resistance.

The JSLIST Block 1 Glove Upgrade Program is seeking an interim glove to replace the current butyl rubber glove.

Manufacturer

National Center for the Employment of the Disabled (El Paso, TX)
Group Home Foundation (Belfast, ME)
Creative Apparel (Belfast, ME)

South Eastern Kentucky Rehabilitation Industries (Corbin, KY)

Peckham Vocational Industries (Lansing, MI)

Battelle (Stafford, VA)

Wheeled Vehicles

Logistics is the ball and chain of armoured warfare.

—German General Heinz Guderian

Logistics are an important part of modern warfare, and the U.S. Army has a variety of wheeled vehicles to support its operations. Most of the vehicles in this section are concerned with logistics, though the HMMWV and Stryker both have combat roles.

Family of Medium Tactical Vehicles (FMTV)

Mission

Fill the Army's medium tactical-vehicle requirements for unit mobility and unit resupply, and transportation of equipment and personnel.

Entered Army Service

1996

Description and Specifications

The Family of Medium Tactical Vehicles (FMTV) is a series of vehicles based on a common chassis, which vary by payload and mission requirements. The LMTV (Light Medium Tactical Vehicle) has a 2.5-ton capacity (cargo and van models). The MTV (Medium Tactical Vehicle) has a 5-ton capacity (cargo and long-wheelbase cargo with and without materiel handling equipment, tractor, van, wrecker, and dump truck models). Three truck variants and two companion trailers, with the same cube and payload capacity as their prime movers, provide air drop capability.

The FMTV replaced older, maintenance-intensive trucks. They perform local and line haul, unit mobility, unit resupply, and other missions in combat, combat support, and combat service support units. It is rapidly deployable worldwide and operates on primary and secondary roads, trails, and cross-country terrain, in all climatic conditions. Commonality of parts across truck chassis variants significantly reduces the logistics burden and operating and support costs. New vehicle applications are being developed to meet new requirements.

The FMTV A1 series includes a 1999 Environmental Protection Agency-certified engine, upgraded transmission, electronic data bus, an anti-lock brake system and interactive electronic technical manuals.

LMTV A1 CARGO

    Payload: 5,000 lbs
    Towed Load: 12,000 lbs
    Engine: JP8 Fuel
    Transmission: Automatic
    Horsepower: 275
    Drive: 4x4

MTV A1 CARGO

    Payload: 10,000 lbs
    Towed Load: 21,000 lbs

Engine: JP8 Fuel
Transmission: Automatic
Horsepower: 330
Drive: 6x6

Manufacturer

Stewart & Stevenson Services, Inc. (Sealy, TX)

Heavy Expanded Mobility Tactical Truck (HEMTT)

Mission

Provide transport capabilities for re-supply of combat vehicles and weapons systems.

Entered Army Service

1982

Description and Specifications

There are five basic configurations of the HEMTT series trucks: M977 cargo truck with Materiel Handling Crane, M978 2,500 gallon fuel tanker, M985 cargo truck with Materiel Handling Crane, M983 tractor and the M984 wrecker. A self-recovery winch is also available on certain models. This vehicle family is rapidly deployable and is designed to operate in any climatic condition where military operations are expected to occur. The HEMTT is the backbone of U.S. Army logistics. Standard features include front and rear tow eyes, blackout lights, 24-volt electrical system, and rear pintle hook for towing trailers and artillery. All models are C130, C141, and C17 air-transportable and are capable of fording water crossings up to 48 inches deep.

The HEMTT Load Handling System (LHS) consists of a standard HEMTT (M977/M978 or M985 chassis) prime mover (8 x 8 foot configuration) equipped with an integral load-handing system providing self-load/unload capability and capable of transporting an 11-ton payload. LHS carries equipment/ammunition/supply loads on demountable "flatrack" cargo beds and is able to tow an 11-ton payload trailer also capable of carrying flatracks. The containerised roll-in/out platform (CROP), an A-frame type flatrack that fits inside a 20-foot International Standards Organisation container, gives the HEMTT LHS added cargo carrying capability. Flatracks and CROPs are interchangeable between HEMTT LHS and the Palletised Load System.

The FMTV A1 series includes a 1999 Environmental Protection Agency-certified engine, upgraded transmission, electronic data bus, an anti-lock brake system and interactive electronic technical manuals.

M977

    Length: 401 in
    Wheelbase: 210 in
    Turning Circle: 100 in
    Weight without Winch: 37,900 lbs
    Weight with Winch: 38,800 lbs
    Width: 96 in

Height: Operational 112 in; Transport 102 in
Ground Clearance: 24 in
Cruising Range: 300 miles at maximum speed
Maximum Grade: 60% with payload of 22,000 lbs
Engine: 445 or 450 horsepower diesel engine
Transmission: 4-speed automatic and 2-speed Oshkosh transfer case with air-operated front tandem axle disconnect
Crew: 2

M978

Length: 401 in
Wheelbase: 210 in
Turning Circle: 100 in
Weight without Winch: 37,300 lbs
Weight with Winch: 38,200 lbs
Width: 96 in
Height: Operational 112 in; Transport 102 in
Ground Clearance: 24 in
Cruising Range: 300 miles at maximum speed
Maximum Grade: 60% with payload of 22,000 lbs
Engine: 445 or 450 horsepower diesel engine
Transmission: 4-speed automatic and 2-speed Oshkosh transfer case with air-operated front tandem axle disconnect
Crew: 2

M985

Length: 401 in

Wheelbase: 210 in
Turning Circle: 100 in
Weight without Winch: 38,700 lbs
Weight with Winch: 39,600 lbs
Width: 96 in
Height: Operational 112 in; Transport 102 in
Ground Clearance: 24 in
Cruising Range: 300 miles at maximum speed
Maximum Grade: 60% with payload of 22,000 lbs
Engine: 445 or 450 horsepower diesel engine
Transmission: 4-speed automatic and 2-speed Oshkosh transfer case with air-operated front tandem axle disconnect
Crew: 2

M983

Length: 351 in
Wheelbase: 181 in
Turning Circle: 91 in
Weight without Crane: 32,200 lbs
Weight with Crane: 39,200 lbs
Width: 96 in
Height: Operational 112 in; Transport 102 in
Ground Clearance: 24 in
Cruising Range: 300 miles at maximum speed
Maximum Grade: 60% with payload of 22,000 lbs
Engine: 445 or 450 horsepower diesel engine

Transmission: 4-speed automatic and 2-speed Oshkosh transfer case with air-operated front tandem axle disconnect

Crew: 2

M984

Length: 392 in
Wheelbase: 191 in
Turning Circle: 95 in
Weight: 50,900 lbs
Width: 96 in
Height: Operational 112 in; Transport 102 in
Ground Clearance: 24 in
Cruising Range: 300 miles at maximum speed
Maximum Grade: 60% with payload of 22,000 lbs
Engine: 445 or 450 horsepower diesel engine
Transmission: 4-speed automatic and 2-speed Oshkosh transfer case with air-operated front tandem axle disconnect

Crew: 2

MANUFACTURER

Oshkosh Truck (Oshkosh, WI)

HMMWV (High Mobility Multi-purpose Wheeled Vehicle)

Mission

Provide a common light tactical vehicle capability. Replaced the quarter-ton jeep, M718A1 ambulance, half-ton Mule, 1.25-ton Gamma Goat, and M792 ambulance.

Entered Army Service

1985

Description and Specifications

The HMMWV is a light, highly mobile, diesel-powered, four-wheel-drive vehicle equipped with an automatic transmission. Based on the M998 chassis, using common components and kits, the HMMWV can be configured to become a troop carrier, armament carrier, S250 shelter carrier, ambulance, TOW missile carrier, and a Scout vehicle.

The M998 is the baseline vehicle for the M998 series of 1 1/4-ton trucks, which are known as the HMMWV vehicles. The HMMWV vehicles include 11 variants. They are:

M998 Cargo/Troop Carrier
M1038 Cargo/Troop Carrier, with winch
M1043 Armament Carrier
M1044 Armament Carrier, with winch
M1045 TOW Carrier
M1046 TOW Carrier, with winch
M997 Ambulance, basic armour 4-Litter
M1035 Ambulance, 2-Litter
M1037 Shelter Carrier
M1042 Shelter Carrier, with winch
M1097 Heavy HMMWV (payload of 4,400 pounds)

All HMMWVs are designed for use over all types of roads, in all weather conditions and are extremely effective in the most difficult terrain. The HMMWV's high power-to-weight ratio, four-wheel drive and high ground clearance combine to give it outstanding cross-country mobility.

Length: 15 ft
Width: 7.08 ft
Height: 6.00 feet reducible to 4.5 feet
Weight: 5,200 lbs
Engine: V8, 6.2 litre displacement, fuel-injected diesel, liquid cooled, compression ignition
Horsepower: 150 at 3,600 RPM

Transmission: 3 speed, automatic
Transfer Case: 2 speed, locking, chain driven
Electrical System: 24 volt, negative ground, 60 amps
Brakes: Hydraulic, 4-wheeled disc
Fording Depth: without preparation: 2.5 ft (76.2 cm); with deep water fording kit : 5 ft (1.5 m)
Fuel Type: Diesel
Fuel Capacity: 25 gallons
Range: 350 mile highway
Max. Speed: 65 mph

Manufacturer

AM General (South Bend, IN)
O'Gara-Hess & Eisenhardt (Fairfield, OH)

M1070 Heavy Equipment Transporter (HET)

Mission

Transport, deploy, recover, and evacuate combat-loaded main battle tanks and other heavy tracked and wheeled vehicles to and from the battlefield.

Entered Army Service

1993

Description and Specifications

The Heavy Equipment Transport System (HETS) consists of the M1070 Truck Tractor and the M1000 Heavy Equipment Transporter Semi-trailer. The HETS transports payloads up to 70 tons – primarily Abrams tanks. It operates on highways worldwide (with permits), secondary roads, and cross-country. The HETS has a number of features that significantly improve the mobility and overall performance of the system in a tactical environment. The M1070 tractor has front- and rear-axle steering, a central tire-inflation system, and cab space for six personnel to accommodate the two HETS operators and four tank crewmen. The M1000 semi-trailer has automatically steerable axles and a load-levelling hydraulic suspension.

    Tractor Length: 358 in
    Tractor Width: 102 in
    Trailer Length: 622 in
    Trailer Width (at rear bumper): 144.8 in
    Tractor Curb Weight: 41,000 lbs
    Trailer Curb Weight: 50,000 lbs
    Payload: 140,000 lbs
    Engine: 500 horsepower Detroit Diesel
    Transmission: 5-speed automatic
    Speed: 40-45 mph on highway (25-30 mph with 70 ton payload)
    Range: 300 mi
    Fording: 28 in
    Air Transportability: C-5A and C-17

Manufacturer

    Tractor: Oshkosh Truck (Oshkosh, WI)
    Trailer: Systems & Electronics, Inc. (St Louis, MO)

Palletised Load System (PLS)

Mission

Perform line haul, local haul, unit resupply, and other missions in the tactical environment to support modernised and highly mobile combat units. Rapid movement of combat-configured loads of ammunition and all classes of supply, shelters, and containers.

Entered Army Service

1993

Description and Specifications

The Palletised Load System (PLS) consists of a prime mover truck with an integral self-loading and unloading capability, a payload trailer (M1076), and demountable cargo beds, referred to as flatracks. The PLS prime mover truck carries its payloads on its demountable flatrack cargo beds, or inside 8 x 8 x 20-ft International Standards Organisation (ISO) containers, or shelters. The PLS prime mover truck comes in two mission-oriented configurations: the M1074 and the M1075. The M1074 is equipped with a variable reach Material Handling Crane (MHC) to support forward-deployed Artillery units. The M1075, without MHC, is used in conjunction with the M1076 trailer in support of transportation line haul missions. The M1076 trailer, capable of carrying payloads up to 16.5 tons, is equipped with a flatrack that is interchangeable between truck and trailer. The prime mover truck and trailer form a self-contained system that loads and unloads its cargo without the need for forklifts or other material handling equipment. Without leaving the cab, the driver can load or unload the truck in less than one minute, and both truck and trailer in less than five minutes.

Two additional pieces of equipment enhance PLS flexibility. The M3 containerised roll-in/out platform (CROP) is an A-frame type flatrack which fits inside a 20-ft ISO container. A container handling unit (CHU) enables PLS to pick up and transport ISO containers without using a flatrack. Flatracks and CROP are interchangeable between PLS and the HEMTT-LHS.

The PLS prime mover features a central tire inflation system that significantly improves off-road mobility. Current NATO agreements require PLS to maintain interoperability with comparable British, German, and French systems through the use of a common flatrack.

PLS is a major enabler of the Army's drive to achieve a distribution-based logistics system. The PLS-Enhanced (PLS-E) program procures the Movement Tracking System (MTS), which provides a multitude of tactical wheeled vehicles with Global Positioning System capability and two-way digital messaging. The MTS enables the commander to track logistics assets over the range of the battle space. The two-way messaging allows redirection of logistics assets as needs develop.

    Truck Payload: 16.5 tons
Trailer Payload: 16.5 tons
Truck Length: 431 in
Trailer Length: 327.4 in (includes trailer tongue, with flatrack)
Truck Width: 96 in
Trailer Width: 95.7 in
Flatrack Dimensions: 8 x 20 ft
Engine Type: 500 horsepower Detroit Diesel
Transmission: Automatic (5-speed forward, 1 reverse)
Number of Driven Wheels: 10
Range: 300 mi
Fording Capability: 48 in
Air Transportability: C-5A, C-17, C-141 (with preparation)
Cab: 2 person

MANUFACTURER

    Truck and CHU: Oshkosh Truck (Oshkosh, WI)
Trailer and Flatrack: Oshkosh Truck (Bradenton, FL)
CROP: Summa Technologies (Huntsville, Al); Hyundai Precision America (San Diego, CA)

STRYKER

MISSION

To fulfil an immediate requirement in the Army's current transformation process to equip a strategically deployable (C-17/C-5) and operationally deployable (C-130) brigade capable of rapid movement anywhere on the globe in a combat-ready configuration. The armoured wheeled vehicle is designed to enable the Stryker Brigade Combat Team (SBCT) to manoeuvre more easily in close and urban terrain while providing protection in open terrain.

ENTERED ARMY SERVICE

May 2002

DESCRIPTION AND SPECIFICATIONS

Stryker comprises two variants – the Infantry Carrier Vehicle (ICV) and the Mobile Gun System (MGS). The ICV has eight additional configurations: Reconnaissance

Vehicle (RV); Mortar Carrier (MC); Commanders Vehicle (CV); Fire Support Vehicle; (FSV); Engineer Squad Vehicle (ESV); Medical Evacuation Vehicle (MEV); Anti-tank Guided Missile Vehicle (ATGM); and NBC Reconnaissance Vehicle (NBCRV).

Performance highlights include C-130 transportability; internetted C4ISR capability; integral all-around 14.5mm armour protection and 152mm artillery air burst protection (upgradeable to Rocket Propelled Grenade (RPG) protection with add-on armour); self-deployment and self-recovery capability; reduced vehicle acoustic signature; ability to carry a nine-man infantry or engineer squad; and bunker and wall breaching capability.

These highlights provide a force that will move rapidly as a cohesive combined arms combat team, a capability not previously present in the Army inventory.

Weight: 19 tons

Power train: Engine similar to that used in Family of Medium Tactical Vehicles (FMTV)

Speed: In excess of 60 mph

Cruising Range: In excess of 300 miles on 53 gallons of fuel

Three block improvements are planned for the Stryker. A crew-installable add-on armour kit that provides 360-degree RPG-7 protection, an internal recoil-mounted 120mm mortar system, and embedded training that will be provided beginning with the third SBCT. Block improvements will be retrofitted to SBCTs 1 and 2 in subsequent years.

Manufacturer

General Dynamics Land Systems

Digital Reinforcements: Free Ebook

To get a free ebook of this title, simply go to www.shilka.co.uk/dr and enter code DEFEND73.

The free ebook can be downloaded in several formats: Mobi (for Kindle devices & apps), ePub (for other ereaders & ereader apps), and PDF (for reading on a computer). Ereader apps are available for all computers, tablets and smartphones.

About Russell Phillips

Russell Phillips writes books and articles about military technology and history. His articles have been published in *Miniature Wargames*, *Wargames Illustrated* and the *Society of Twentieth Century Wargamers' Journal*. Some of these articles are available on his website.

To get a free book and advance notice of new books, join Russell's mailing list at www.rpbook.co.uk/freebook. You can unsubscribe at any time.

Word of mouth is crucial for any author to succeed. If you enjoyed this book, please consider leaving a review where you bought it, or on a site like Goodreads. Even a short review would be very much appreciated.

Also by Russell Phillips

Red Steel: Soviet Tanks and Combat Vehicles of the Cold War

A Fleet in Being: Austro-Hungarian Warships of WWI

The Bear Marches West: 12 Scenarios for 1980s NATO vs Warsaw Pact Wargames

A Damn Close-Run Thing: A Brief History of the Falklands Conflict

FIND RUSSELL PHILLIPS ONLINE

Website: www.rpbook.co.uk
Twitter: @RPBook
Facebook: facebook.com/RussellPhillipsBooks
Google Plus: google.com/+RussellPhillips
E-mail: russell@rpbook.co.uk
Join Russell's mailing list: www.rpbook.co.uk/freebook

Made in the USA
San Bernardino, CA
01 February 2017